THE BRIGHTEST THING

Caitlin Press Inc.
8100 Alderwood Road,
Halfmoon Bay, BC V0N 1Y1
www.caitlin-press.com

Text and cover design by Vici Johnstone
Cover illustration: Virginia Frances Sterrett
Printed in Canada

Caitlin Press Inc. acknowledges financial support from the Government of Canada and the Canada Council for the Arts, and the Province of British Columbia through the British Columbia Arts Council and the Book Publisher's Tax Credit.

Library and Archives Canada Cataloguing in Publication

Daniell, Ruth, 1987-, author
     The brightest thing / Ruth Daniell.
Poems.
ISBN 978-1-987915-90-7 (softcover)

     I. Title.

PS8607.A55665B75 2019   C811'.6   C2018-905972-9

THE BRIGHTEST THING

by
Ruth Daniell

CAITLIN PRESS

for Mom, Dad, Darrell & James — with my love & gratitude

Contents

III Learning to Be Two

IV Blue Moon

I
Fairy Tales

On the Bicentennial of the Grimm Brothers'
Kinder-und Hausmärchen

Long before the house in Cassel,
where they collected fairy tales into manuscripts,
they were boys in the rural village of Steinau.
They loved to collect the eggs from their family's hens.
Most other chores were seen as interruptions
to their studies but they liked to collect the eggs.
It doesn't seem so surprising to me. I remember
collecting eggs at my great grandfather's farm:
I was never sure they would be there,
tucked in the nests, though I had reason to hope.
Finding the eggs was a real pleasure,
handing them into someone else's hands,
still warm, and trusting that something good
would be made with them.

Family Portrait: Medieval Times, Buena Park, CA

I.

At dinner we'll have roasted chicken leg
dressed up as baby dragon and the waitress
will introduce herself as our serving wench
and a choreographed jousting tournament
will kick up sawdust in the castle's arena,
the horse's hooves interrupting the princess
singing in her stage tower—
                                                    We're fairy tale, too,
because my father sprang for the King's
Royalty Package. It comes with first-row seating,
knight's cheering banners, a behind-the-scenes DVD,
commemorative program and a framed group photo,
which he upgrades for us upon arrival to include costumes.
The photo studio assistants with their bland name tags
address me and my mother as "m'lady,"
usher us to roll racks of tasselled robes.
"Here's our selection for queens,"
someone says to Mom. "You can choose
your princess dress here," they say to me.
No questions asked. We are who we are.
Someone adjusts my beaded tiara. My mother
touches her crown, radiant with gold
glitter. The room with its green screen
is thick with the kind of magic that gilds
the memory of my fiancé and my brother,
two princes choosing prop swords
off a studio wall, laughing wide-mouthed
like lions on a crest—

II.

Mom and I are in the front of the frame. Ladies
first. Beneath all the purple velvet, bronze brocade,
we're still wearing jeans. I can see my fiancé's
black-and-white-striped Adidas Gazelles
under his prince's robes.
My brother, twenty-two and cool, determined
that *if we're gonna do this, we're gonna do it right*,
doesn't smile for the camera, but relaxes
his face as if he's come from battle.
Above his blood-red cape,
the T-shirt I bought him three Christmases ago.
It's hard to believe in his dragons.
The two princes' swords sparkle
in pixels above us, in an enchanted forest
with its too-good-to-be true waterfall
and dappled fairy light. In the centre,
here's Dad: six foot six, mid-fifties, capable
of giving his grown family a holiday
on an indulgent budget.
A man who chose California,
who chose Disneyland, who chose
Medieval Times. When they dressed him,
the studio assistants reached for
the largest king's crown,
but my father chose, neglected on the prop table,
a clown's hat. "I want to be the jester,"
he said. In the photo it's the brightest thing.

Fire and Safety

(or, *If my little brother is jumping out of helicopters into raging flames I don't
want to know about it*)

Your days against the fires, nights — guilty,
gold and red against the dark trees — glitter
in the periphery of my heart. The blur is
deliberate. I want you safe — explosions
in front of you on the TV in our parents'
basement, the orange, red and
brown knitted afghan bunched at one end
of the couch, your laptop a flat heat
against your stomach and your eyes closed
against the insomnia of your childhood
bed, your lashes curled like floating
ash. Empty Coke cans, bags of chips,
silver linings in the dim electronic light.

Close up, in photographs I never asked to see,
the clouds are mirrors, the fire
a deep red. I've always felt
vermillion was a reptilian word: the smoke billows
are snakes, you find small lizards
in the aching moss, even the dry needles slither
somehow. The fire smacks its lips,
clucks its many tongues —

Dead trees need to be felled. You explain
that you've come to have a relationship
with your chainsaw: she knows your hands,
you've come to understand her — her shivers
and starts, the peculiar whine
when she needs attention. Third season
with the same saw. It is a kind of fidelity
I'm uncomfortable to learn. The first time
I tried to tell you I was in love, needed

to tell someone—you cut me off, afraid
I was going to say something about sex
you didn't want to know. There are some things,
you tried to teach me, we shouldn't know
about each other. I'm a virgin until
I tell you otherwise. You're safe
until you tell me you're not.

Fairy Tales

Alone at lunch hour I lie down on the field
lined with wild roses and rainwater and search
through the grasses until I can almost see them
hiding in the weeds. Just a few centimetres tall
and very quick, they begin to follow me
whenever I am alone. And I am alone everywhere
except at home, where you and I share every game,
every discovery, and so I explain that I know them:
they are tiny, they don't have wings but their skins are gold,
and their miniature shirts and vests and hats and shoes
and dresses and coats are gold, and their eyelashes are gold,
and their eyes are black as coal. And you, amazed, squint
at the shadow beneath the mountain ash in the front yard.
You're sure you can see them too.

Then, older, you're sure you can kill them.
You try stomping on them and throwing things at them
but I always inform you they've just moved,
they weren't in that spot, can't you see them anymore?
Maybe you can't. Maybe you're angry. Maybe
you're hurt. Maybe you were lied to and magic
isn't real. But years later in a toast to the bride,
you admit you've asked them for forgiveness
and they've agreed to come to your sister's wedding.
Suddenly the dance floor is gold
with imaginary friends.

Love and IKEA

I like the twangy earnestness of old country songs.
You have a soft spot for '80s power ballads.
I catch you singing falsetto in the shower.
I want to know what love is: your short blond hair
lathered into a mohawk I muss up
when I step under the water. Our lives are full
of happy clichés, mismatched music,
misplaced socks, IKEA furniture—
the bookcase designed without spacers
that offends your handyman sensibility.
Everybody has baseboards, you say,
hitting the birch-effect veneer with the flat of your hand.
Later, when you smack your head
on the as-yet-unsecured *piece of shit pressboard*
you can't find any Band-Aids but the Disney ones
you bought me months ago.
You return from the medicine cabinet fuming
and wearing a pink Little Mermaid on your forehead.
Someone must have said everything about this before—
about anger transformed into hilarity, about hearts
drawn in the steam of the glass shower door, and singing.

Love and Photography

            The banana slugs
by the Sooke Potholes are sloppy, slow
long vowels we tread lightly around,
side by side on the path's blue and white gravel,
beside the river's white water whooshing into the would-be
corners of rock. The last time we spoke,
you told me you were gay, and cried,
because this isn't what you wanted to be.
No one else knows. And now,
we find a slug sliced through, translucent
as watermelon flesh, a bicycle tire's harsh soft mark,
and you don't want to talk about it. You can't
take it back. The trees are almost neon with moss
and the sky a shredded denim-blue. It all nicely sets off
my purple coat, you say, your camera lens widening
to take in the colours I can't name exactly. You ask me why
I haven't written a poem for you, if it's because
sorrow fuels art and you haven't caused me any,
if it's because we never dated — why didn't we date? —
did I know this thing about you before you did?
Can I tell just by looking at you?
                        I rarely feel so seen
as when you're taking my photograph
but I don't know what to tell you.
Hearts are almost always invisible, our bodies opaque.
Tonight, we'll drive back into town,
pick my boyfriend up from work. He's your friend,
too; he will look at your sad face and know
not to ask anything. The three of us
will get drunk and when it's 3 a.m.
we'll buy Doritos and Mars bars
from the corner store, pretend we're sober
so the cashier will be polite to us, then wander
Cook Street until we reach the ocean, indistinguishable
from the black sky with our naked eyes,
everything darker than your secret.

Little Brother

I hate how the summers take you out of cell service range—
weeks go by with no words on what your day-to-day life is like
and I imagine you long-legged up those mountains,
sap sweetening the slivers of skin between your gloves
and the cuffs of your government-issued, flame-resistant shirt.
In the fairy tale, the siblings run away from the witch
but she flings spells at their small backs and they run,
growing thirsty, through the darkening trees.
Little Brother takes a sip from an enchanted stream
and transforms into a deer, whose first instinct is to run
away from his sister—but she undoes her golden garter,
collars him, leads him with her deeper into the forest. He wants
to stay with her, but the animal of him can't help it—
he needs to run when he hears the sounds of horns
and the king's hunt. *They'll never catch me*,
he says, and Little Sister cannot keep him
leashed. I want to stay home; I am afraid of everything
so I don't understand the way you leap into the forest,
year after year, to fight those fires, but
faith, like soft-felted antlers, grows slowly, is a kind of armour,
and so far you've always come back.

I've never read a love poem

in which the couple is sitting in the proctologist's office.
It is not a grand place for love. The man shyly shuffles
through the magazines on the long low table
until he finds a slender copy of an old comic book:
Dr. Bruce Banner's wedding to his long-time girlfriend
Betty is interrupted by gunshots; in a few pages his fear
will stretch him into the Hulk and the dearly beloved
will scatter into their Ben-Day dots. Cyan, magenta,
yellow, black. The receptionist calls him into
this clean white room with the woman
sitting beside him, her hands clasped in front of her.
He follows her name into the examination room,
can't help wondering out loud, *How many butts*
do you think the doctor touches a day? The medical charts
on the walls are full of tediously earnest illustrations.
There were a lot of other patients in the waiting room.
Do you think he touches twenty a day? Thirty?
He follows her eyes to stare at the white tile floor.
The doctor arrives matter-of-factly, succinct, asks brisk
questions about the woman's pain, asks her
to lie on her side, raise her skirt, then slides
an imaging instrument into her rectum, rummages
around. The man looks away
or he does not and it does not matter.

After, the woman tries to stand, but pain stops her.
She feels her body pulled from her darkest places
as if by a hook, a piece of wire fence twisted by a thug,
some comic book minion. The man watches
the colour of her face drain away and he reaches for her.
The doctor leaves and the woman lies down
on the tissue-papered table again, curls up,
balls herself up like a Kleenex. The man rests
a large warm hand on the woman's back.
He can't hear her crying but he can feel her spine shudder.

The man looks away or he does not. His hand rises and falls
with her breath, dearly beloved, and they are Ben-Day dots:
the separate instances of themselves,
when viewed at even a small distance,
come together in one image — the lines
between their bodies are bright and blurry
against the grand scheme of things, the comic life.

Waiting for Spring, or Something

When I read to a child a poem with a death in it,
she asked what *bury* means. I explained
that when people die sometimes we dig
a hole and we put them inside it. The child
told me that's wrong. You shouldn't put people
in the ground. You should put them in heaven.
For months now I've been regretting shovels,
imagining, instead, a crane lifting bodies
directly into the clouds. Outside
our apartment, a machine moves
concrete slabs from one place
to another—its tall yellow latticed boom
seemly in the sky but its reach finite.
The solstice is bringing the light back
but it takes so long. Epiphany
comes uncomfortably into my winter
body: if heaven's anywhere it's not
here. It might not even be
a place, it might be moments, my ideal
state of being already *was* – playing
video games in my parents' basement
with you and my brother and our best friend Matt
and the smell of the wood stove and the smoke-
coloured suede couch stuffed with mismatched pillows
and the green-and-yellow-tasselled football blanket
and fairy lights winding Christmas up the stairs' railing.
I don't want my dad to die, the child said.
I don't want my mom to die. I don't want,
she said, *anyone to die.* I put the poem away.
Grey flickered into grey and now the evenings
fray with slightly longer light. At the altar
I promised that I would need no home but the one I found
in you but, sweetheart, I'm still sad here in the city's
never-ending construction, its building and babble.
In the town where I grew up someone I know is dying.

Everyone I know will die. I'm waiting
for the lift of love's machinery, for the crane
with creaks and sighs to settle me
through the clouds into our impossible, near past.

You're Living in a Big City Now

At nine o'clock at night you're looking down.
No footprints on the indiscriminate sidewalks,
cigarette butts like discarded stars on its wet sky,
uneven pavement. Paper cups dribble coffee
into the creases where the weeds aren't even trying
to be beautiful. Gravel scuffed by heels into streaks,
grains of a comet's tail brushing unhappy against
another world. You hate this place all day long,
finally arrive at your apartment, check your email.
Your mother's been figuring out her new iPhone.
She's taken a picture of the moon
in the front yard of the house where you grew
up. It's hanging above the cul-de-sac
between the street light and the mountain ash tree
and you know just where she must have been standing
to get that moon just so. You can almost see her
silhouette reaching from the front porch,
the clip of cedar beside the steps, the things
the picture leaves out. But the moon. It's in your inbox.
Here. If you bother to look you'll see it whole and
unhurt above your apartment window, too, this city's streets.
The moon is everywhere but all you can think is you're not home.

Folk Tale Type 425C

You have had quite enough of the Louvre,
although you do admit to liking the statues
of Cupid and Psyche. The young god's wings
don't look as if they could really hold him up
but he reaches a hand towards the woman
about to lift her mouth near his. They are almost kissing,
transcendent with desire, and I explain to you
that they are the precursors to Beauty and her Beast.
Tale type 425C appears across cultures to express
anxiety about marriage and the complexities of love.
Jeanne-Marie Leprince de Beaumont made the story famous
when she published it in France in 1756 and emphasized
gratitude instead of passion within love. The wingless
Beast doesn't arch his back, like Cupid does, in anticipated pleasure
over his soft-breasted love: instead he gives thanks,
gives thanks, gives thanks. *Thanks for not insisting*
we stay any longer, you say, rubbing your sore back.
I think of the long stone museum floors and the vertebra
you damaged by falling out of a second-storey window
when you were seven. The story has many variants.

II
The Princess Who Felt the Pea

Briar Rose

It was the strangest sensation: my blood
seemed to rush like a waterfall backwards
from my fingertip, a skein of flax unwinding

into the basket of my heart, pooled and knotty
and fifteen. The spindle sharp as sleep
jerked away from me by sudden touch:

his lips static against mine. But first:
my parents arriving too late in the great hall
from some royal errand more urgent

than their daughter. But perhaps they knew
they had nothing to unravel the tight-knit curse,
and they could not stand to watch my eyes close,

like that, into dreams about the castle doves,
waking a hundred years later with broken wings.

Lavinia

after William Shakespeare's *Titus Andronicus*

I.

He caught my hand in my father's garden—
closed flowers quiet in the earth, dusk,
the horizon blue and yellow together
without mixing into green.
I wanted that, for us to touch
without blending into one thing.

When Bassianus lifted my face to his,
kissed me, I felt the crocuses grow
curious. Later, the light
slipped out of the sky,
and though my father was gone to war,
the emperor buried,
I found I could lie awake without worry,
the familiar scent of earth
suddenly a new memory, a seed,
something upturned.

II.

Betrothed: I
kept the word in my mouth, round
as an olive, and it ripened
with thought: green,
then purple. My soft nipples
strange coins, my body treasured
and untouched —
the quiet blue vines of my blood
growing warm,
imagining otherwise.

III.

Like something removed
from my heart, the drums
announced my father's arrival.
I saw the soldiers' burden:
stretcher and stretcher of covered bodies,
my brothers wrapped in grey,
cocooned and flightless.

I rushed forward,
lifted my dress above my ankles.
And as I passed by
the tribunes and officials,
Saturninus turned his head.
I felt his eyes follow me,
let my skirts drop to the ground.
The road's dust shape-shifted
at my feet—first one thing,
then another.

IV.

The three men's voices were sharp,
cutting across desire and entitlement
as a switchback cuts across torn grass
and hard rock. My father
listened and talked and listened.
Saturninus wanted me. Bassianus had me.
I was the weather, a topic of conversation,
ordinary, observed, matter-of-fact — but if I was
weather, I wanted to be its mystery, too,
wanted the strength of the seasons, the voice
of the wind. When Bassianus glanced at me
I knew he remembered the independence of the moon,
the sun, the rain. He couldn't control when water fell
but he would hold it cool in his hands
when it came.

The Swans' Sister

To save my brothers, six
shirts sewn of asters and six years without
speaking. No laughing, either,
the magic said: but that was only hard
in spring, watching the new animals
learn to stand — lambs and foals wobbling
like the silent o my mouth made in the moat's
reflection. I stood at the water and unclenched
my jaw and wondered what to make of the husband
who wed me, voiceless. He had found me hidden in a tree,
clutching swan feathers to my chest.
He called up, *Who, Who*
are you? like an owl questioning his dark self.
I was always listening for birds. Every time
the king came to me at night, I worried
the unfriendly magic would hear my gasps,
or the sound of my thoughts, my king's name
on the edge of my tongue in the silk
of my bed. Mornings filled the windows
with wings and I thought of my brothers,
the asters somehow never wilting
as I worked, though it took all those years
to tame those purple petals, those stems
reminding me of the handmade crowns my brothers
bent during our shared childhood of fields,
flowers, the songs we used to sing —
Now I would not utter even my prayers and so
my king's mother decided I must be a witch.
I shook my head, no, as visions of water
beading off a shaken wing lit in my head.
Still I would not speak. Their long ivory necks
and beating blood. I finished all six shirts but
the left sleeve of the last arm.
Led to the stake — the queen mother's accusations
unabated, the king's doubt

no longer nocturnal, his eyes on my lips —
I carried the shirts draped over my arms,
over the loose sleeves of my disgraced
queen's robe. Standing on the stack of wood,
I distracted myself by looking for spiders
in amongst the kindling, admired the knots
that told me where the tree had once
twisted toward more light, circling
shadow — and then the shadows were white
wings above me, and hope swooped in.
I threw the shirts over my brothers
and watched the asters touch them,
the swan skins fall off. My brothers
before me, human, handsome
and vigorous. My youngest brother
missing his left arm. His one swan wing
shining with new uselessness
and all my unspoken love.

The Third Eldest Sea Princess

I.

I spun out and up — my fish tail adorned
with six oyster shells, my mark as princess —
and swam further than anyone else,
followed a wide river inland, learned the greenness
of hills full of grapevines, saw castles,
manor houses that glinted silver between trees.
Grandmother had told us about birds
but they were stranger than I had imagined —
softer. A tame duck let me pet it, its feathers
not like scales but closer to the silk of seaweed,
undisturbed sand. Water beaded off the bird's back,
its emerald neck. Its eyes were surprisingly dark:
everything would be brighter, I had thought,
this close to the sun, a yellow jellyfish
suspended in clear blue. I watched the duck
blink its eyes and flash its beak. Other birds,
some of them small, flitting like minnows,
floated from branch to branch.
And one large, slate-blue creature —
what Grandmother had described once,
called *heron*. It lifted its wings into the air and
I felt the same hush claim me
as I felt listening to a whale's song. Yes,
I thought, this world is good.

Inland, a group of naked children cooling themselves
at the riverbank, voices weightless above the water
and I felt my heart hush again, sound shimmering
as I drew near, as I had approached the duck, slow
and careful, wonder blooming in me like ink in water,
dark and un-dangerous... But when they saw me,
the children cried out. Monster,
I dove away, knowing that world
was closed to me, as near as breath and impossible.

II.

We all kept gardens.
I spent whole days gathering blue stones,
waiting for the whale songs,
whispers and the lull of home.
But I also caught myself
straining to hear the surface —
our white-fingered world reaching out
for the coarse sand, then retreating
into itself. There. The water
in my hair suddenly something
I could compare to wind —
I didn't want to talk about it
but our little sister hovered
in my peripheral vision,
rearranging red flowers
to resemble the sun
she'd never seen.

III.

Seeing it for herself didn't help. The sun.
I watched her grow slenderer
with longing — could feel her listening
beyond silences
for the improbable noise of the sky.
She let the careful circle
of her garden overflow
with flowers. The red light
seemed to do what cannot be done
to a mermaid: it drowned her,
rippled into her lungs
and long sighs,
tinged her dark tail
pink, almost soft-looking,
skin —

IV.

Jealous and reverent, the others said our little sister's voice
was the most beautiful in the sea, but I wondered
if hers wasn't the loveliest because we heard it the least—
quiet thing, her song so seldom, so spare.
It didn't reach across like the whale's wide songs.
It reached up, away from us, hard and clear and
brittle as the bones the scavengers leave naked
on the ocean floor, just one part of something small
that's gone.

I cried with her because she knew the splendour
of dark ships, stars and storms, and I knew
what want was, a dull ache for something vast.
But hers was a sharper pain.
She wanted the specific beauty of a man
and I could not help her.

The witch's keen magic parted her tail
into the legs of the bride she had to be
to live: his wife, or dead with the first sunlight
after his wedding to another. I found her
that first morning, settled on shore, the potion drunk,
a pink-stoned castle glaring on a bright green hill.
Her tongue cut out as paid gold
for the spell that gave her human legs.
Her oyster shells, ornament of our royal
status, lay discarded amongst the rocks. I snapped
them onto my tail beside my own. They pinched.
I swam away, anger or sadness or its sister searing
through each strong flick of my tail.

V.

My tongueless, kissless sister, decorating
his wedding ship with her soft fingers, would fail
at dawn. I could not have her die for something
I did not believe was love: the sea
witch did not want my tongue, my trickling voice.
She cut off my long dark hair. I travelled to the surface, new
knife in my girlish fist: if my sister stabbed the prince
in the heart, his warm blood would drip onto her feet
and they would grow together into a fish tail and she could live.
The prince's ship gleamed like polished tiger's eye, strewn
with paper and lanterns, the wrong bride asleep against
the embroidered pillows. I lifted the knife to the deck's railing
where my sister leaned her white arms and watched the red
stripe of the sun grow like a meadow of sea marigolds.
For one moment, when she accepted the knife, I hoped —
and then she looked at me and I saw she was clear-headed
with torture, tranquil. I brought my hands to my head,
bald as rock, and sank through the diamond foam.

VI.

Our home was no less beautiful
after our sister's death: the coral walls still stretched
up amongst the ribbony sea plants. The castle roof
was not missing even one of its many seashells,
and they still opened and closed with the flow of the water,
fluttering like eyelids: inside each of them, a pearl,
a miniature milky un-mourning globe.
My window, like all, of the clearest amber,
tall, and arched, and when I opened it
little fishes flittered inside like the birds I could not help
but compare them to, now. They ate out of my hands.
Let themselves be petted. Swam
through the soft turquoise branches
of the palace trees and into the little garden
my little sister coaxed into a circle of red flowers
she imagined looked like the sun.

Now I tended her garden.
The scarlet flowers, the crimson weeping willow
that cast purple shadows on the blue sand—
the slightest ripple stirred the petals, the leaves,
to movement, and I remembered what it was like
to feel the water gently pull my hair behind me
like the wind that accompanied the light
that killed her. My hair never grew back.

The White Bear's Bride

What I remember most is how cold the air was
the day I left my father's house. The air was so cold
there was no snow; it was a clear, solid blue that seemed
to rustle a little as if the sky was a huge curtain
draped from the hidden mechanics of stars and beams.
I could almost see the folds of fabric
swaying, imagined if I went to its edge I might find
gold tassels lightly touching the ground. Life was
actually like that, a little, once I got to the castle:
my bed was rich with silken sheets and curtains
with tassels that quivered, ever so slightly, like icicles
at the edge of a roof. When the unknown man
came into my bed, I misunderstood
the protocols of enchantment. I stayed awake,
silently counting the gold tassels of that great bed,
and remembered how cold the air was the day I left
my father's house. It was so cold there was no snow;
the air was a clear, solid blue, a pure cold
that entered me sharp and soft at the same time.
I breathed deep and felt every atom
of my heart and hands, fingers and cuticles,
the cracks of my lips, creases at the edge of my eyes
where no tears came, my eyelashes, my nose hairs
freezing with each new breath. My legs squeezed
the soft fur of the bear who carried me away.
His great white shoulders rumbling like mountains,
like mountains covered with snow, and moving.

Donkeyskin

My father mourned my mother like a man
eager to put the business behind him.
He left me to make what I could of grief.
The goldfish swam undisturbed. Dragonflies

mated, aerobatic lovers jewelled and joined
in the air. Hummingbirds arrows
targeting sugar. The exotic birds
Mother had loved parroted her last words

around the lake. I was not afraid. I was sad.
I lay on the grass and stared at the sun
until even when I closed my eyes
I could see nothing but light,

and if its imprint left me before
I could sleep, I would stare at the moon
until my eyelids seemed coated
with soft white dust. And I stared, too,

at the blue and black sky iridescent
with silver stars. I did not wish upon them.
There were months like these. And then
my father remembered me. Noticed me.

Noticed my hair as golden as Mother's
or more so. He came up to me in the garden
and circled his two hands around my waist.
Panted praises in my ear. I pushed him

away. His arms strong, tense as the chains
that let the drawbridge down. The castle gates
opening and closing at his command. His voice severe
beside the lake and the promising birds.

The Frog Princess

The golden ball, simple plaything, dear to me
because I imagined it into a sun—
the careful filigree of flames free
of heat but that from my own hands: None
of those dangers I dreamed came near.
But I could still imagine them, throw
the ball in the air, catch it, reach into fear
as if it were a story I could learn. Low
hope: the golden ball dropped into the pool,
suddenly crystal with my future. Last
look into the deepness of the day cool
with shadow and a promise made fast
and loose and desperate: *Anything you
want,* and he wanted me. Water-lurker,
splish-splasher, he knew darkness, blue,
nothing of gold, the sun, my fire; worker
of words and mad wishes, textured, green,
he knew something inside me was mean.

Perhaps he forgot. Or he forgave that flaw
because it was a means to an end,
the spell squashed out of him. I was only awe:
I watched the enchantment ascend,
a golden circle, a pattern of light, a train
of fire spreading like thin cloth—lace
falling round my body, leaning like rain
into the wind, pushing my face to his face
for that first kiss. And that *was* the first.
I have not forgotten the order of things.
The magic that trapped him knew the worst
of me: I threw his body, broke it, a king's

body, a frog's. My violence returned
him to himself.
            The marriage was a good one,
I think. I set aside the golden ball, learned
to love other kinds of imagined fire, sun,
desire. Almost murder, what I had done,
but we only thought of what we won.

The Giantess

My kitchen smelled of the blood
of Englishmen, boys come from
the quiet earth below. Fee fi fo fum.

Oxen, cattle, an entire v of geese
strung out like a necklace of onyx,
their strangled harmonics

wrung out in dark notes, rivulets
on the stained wooden slab.
Block to chop. Knife to stab.

Breakfasts of sausage, veal,
lamb for lunch, a wide-eyed goat
still bleating, a flutter in the throat

before it poured out its silly life,
and I called my man to our table.
Whatever he caught, I was able

to skin it, dress it, clean it, cook.
I don't know why I could do this.
Not for his grumble, the kiss

he gave before stumbling out
to terrorize the farmland below
with his voice, mean and low,

and his appetite for meat.
I liked living in the clouds,
the soft white wisps, crowds

of rain waiting to fall below us,
never on us—just sunshine,
the moon. All that light was mine.

And he was mine. I was useful,
preparing meals for him, doing housework,
tending to every craving and quirk.

He never brought vegetables home.
No cabbage, no carrots, potatoes to wash,
no cucumber, not one squash,

nor green peas on vines. Just
furred bodies shiny
with sweat and intelligence, whiny

pink tongues and plaintive eyes.
He stole things that lived like him.
The beast of his body, limb

to limb taller than any church
we might have married in.
It was, I know, a life of sin.

Still, the size of the hole he left!
The clouds parted for his shoulder,
he thundered down that green stalk, a boulder

shifted free by a loose pebble,
that hapless Jack. Fee fi fo fum.
My giant fell to the earth he came from.

The iron smell of blood remained
on my kitchen table, and the knife
I used to prepare — the rest of my life —

meals for one: green beans, quiet.
A solitary, simple diet.

The Princess Who Felt the Pea

I was the kind of tired that brings on a certain
keenness, a clarity of vision or a sixth sense.
Across the breakfast table, the queen
held a slender, polished spoon in one hand.
I knew she must see herself upside down
inside it, lifting and lowering from the china
bowls translucent as the throats of baby birds:
the thought transported me, briefly, to the wild nests
I found at home. I looked across the table linens,
bleached white, and wondered a little,
uncertainly, at their extravagance:
the unsullied brightness lay creaseless
across the mahogany, and, glowing
faintly like a broken star, was a crystal pitcher
full of freshly squeezed orange juice,
the kind of thing I had never seen
in my mother's breakfast room.
Its shadow stained the tablecloth
like sunlight: a paradox glimmering
like the prince's face suspended above
his morning furs. He was at once obvious
and completely unknown to me. My own
body, now, felt like a wobbling bird to me;
I thought I could warble in the flowing gown
one of the maids had dressed me in
when I first rose out of that ridiculous bed —
twenty mattresses, twenty featherbeds —
for the garment had long, embroidered sleeves
that made my arms feel like graceless wings
and so it did not surprise me at all
when I realized I'd knocked over
the tall-stemmed glass of orange juice
beside my silver plate: of course I had,
of course I had ruined this chance,
my father's best chance at giving me

a life sweet as orange juice
and smooth as white linens.
I apologized for my clumsiness —
I am sorry, I do not think I am quite awake —
and the prince looked up from his bowl
of raspberries. His lips were stained a deep pink,
his mouth parted in a small *o. Did you not sleep well?*
the queen asked, smiling encouragingly,
shaking a white lace napkin. It looked a little
like a dove coming to land, lightly, on her lap.

Beauty

From my tower window, the garden glossy as glass,
a cathedral window laid flat in his courtyard.
Up close, the roses thick with prayer: *I want*
to go home. But what home was
was changing. The castle had no mirrors

or still water. He could not stand to see himself.
My face was disturbed by the unquiet water
of the garden pools I stared into. Everywhere
roses slow and rich as honey or amber or blood.
I practiced gratitude amongst the blooms.

The castle granted me every wish almost
before I thought it except for my wish to leave it.
He granted that request, his eyebrows deep
with dread. I left him for my father's house,
thinking it was still home. I returned

to the castle knowing different, searched for him
in every room, knowing somehow he had been
dying from my absence. I saved him.
After the wedding, I wondered if the match
would have been the same if he had been the one

tasked to hear past the enchantment — if
it had been my voice stuck in the throat
of a beast, my requests for love rumbling
out like threats. I could not hear past my own
prayers at first, the roses muttering after

me, but I came to understand his heart
through the eyes he wore as an animal. I was
willing to look at ugliness, listen to an unmusical love.
I wished I could know he would have done the same
for me. I had been so easy to love, so visible

in the ornate gowns the ladies-in-waiting
insisted upon. That day I found him almost
dying in the garden, I wore my heart on my sleeves
and sewn in diamonds across my bodice,
rustling down my skirts like rain beading off a stem.

Rapunzel

i. Mother Gothel

I knew only one human being:
the one who taught me to call her Mother,
who each day brought me bread, butter,
fresh goat cheese, boiled egg — my well-being
brought each noon as apricot, as peelings
of apple, pear, the juice of plums. And other
things: from twenty ells up, the sound of her
voice; then, the sound of her body freeing

its breath as she pulled my hair tight to my scalp
again, into the braids she twisted like a spell
in her strong hands. In the stone tower above
the swooning lake and fragrant grass, no help,
no language except hers: our days fell
heavy as gold with no one else to love.

ii. The Tower

Those heavy days with no one else to love,
Mother kept me to herself, safe in stone-
curved walls: in the tower, almost alone,
I knew the walnut tree, the pines, pigeon, dove,
blackbird, lark, sparrow, hawk — above
the wildflowers' air, the company of blown
dust and feathers. Daylight and the drone
of wings. Once, a colony of ants. A kind of

happiness even without her, the vines
keeping the warmth inside my small stone room
at night. I knew them, too, the sounds they made
growing as the moon drew its silver lines
across their leaves, the audible velvet gloom
of the stems wrenching together into a braid.

iii. The Prince

Three stems wrenched together like a braid:
Mother, the prince and me. After so much time,
it felt almost like fate—watching him climb
into my room. Dusk. I was so afraid
that first meeting, seeing the light fade
behind his body. His boots a faint chime
against the stone. The moon sudden, sublime
on his unfamiliar face: I swayed,

tuneless, and he told me he was a prince.
I did not know what a man was. He touched
my wrist and my breath caught, my senses agreeing
he was new and real. I blinked hard and winced
as he fingered my hair loose, clutched
me, told me we were only one being.

III
Learning to Be Two

Hans Christian Andersen's Self-Portraits

He was the snowman
melting from love of a stove, the one-legged tin soldier
never revered by the music box ballerina. In 1836,
his unrequited love for Edvard Collin sunk him
into despair, hyperbole and diamonds.
While Edvard held his wedding on the mainland,
Hans hid on the island of Fyn and wrote
"The Little Mermaid": he cast himself into the water
of the story, pious and unalterable—each step
an attempt at winning a soul and full of the pain
of a thousand knives cutting into soft-skinned feet.
A witch cuts out the Little Mermaid's tongue
so she can never tell her prince that she loves him.
Andersen was mute, too, but he kept walking,
a peculiar grace to his unhandsome gait.
His contemporaries say he was a funny looking man:
big nose, comically large hands out of which with silver scissors
he crafted remarkably delicate paper dolls.
He gave the intricate designs to friends.
No two cut-outs were the same. But they had recurring figures:
jumping Pierrots, ballerinas, monsters and beasts and birdcages,
swans and storks atop trees, bootjacks and butterflies,
angels and goblins, cupolas and towers,
flowers, soldiers and staircases and gallows
with hung men holding their flat hearts.

Dust

Most of the time it's easiest for her to think of it
as an isolated, unexpected event—one evening
when he got a little carried away—instead of a long history
feeling his hands where she didn't want them, her hands
where she didn't want them: his voice coaxing her,
past curfew, to keep going, please, if she really cared
she would stay a little longer, she would not leave him
wanting. It's almost easiest to remember the night he finally
pushed himself into her because
there were times before that when his fingers
were as sharp, times she bled, so many times he pressed her
hands around him. She would wait for his mouth
to stop kissing her, to slacken,
for his body to sink into his bed, the wet
spot widening on the comforter and slick
across her fingers. Books had taught her
that being with someone made you feel beautiful
but she didn't feel beautiful. She felt ugly.
He told her what they were doing
wasn't wrong because they were in love,
but she would drive home over the speed limit
through the fog of Foothills Blvd, her skin
crawling with the tiny bacteria she knew were living
there, the dead skin cells shifting off her shoulders
she worried belonged to him. Most of dust
is human skin; she was cobwebs, filthy,
balled up, drifting into the corners no one could reach
to clean.

Learning to Be Two

Loneliness in Two Parts

I.

One day it occurs to her that the act of love
might not be a gift he stole
but might, in fact, never have been precious at all.
She cannot decide which is worse: loss,
or lack misinterpreted as loss.
She remembers the photographs he sent her
of his penis, risen, apparently, with thoughts of her
that she now understands were not about her at all
but about some loneliness he was desperate to force
from himself. How she came to be beneath his eyes
that winter evening had something to do,
also, with loneliness — loneliness thawed
and frozen, thawed and frozen
like snow that no longer resembles itself,
soft slush twisted by careless footprints,
kicked up into shards that freeze again
and sharpen. She remembers that, too:
how sharp he felt inside her,
how the ceiling lamp hummed
over the bed. She wanted to cry out
but couldn't. Darkness found her mouth
in the fluorescent room. He lifted her wrists
above her and pressed through the white noise
of the light.

II.

September afternoon:
you drive us over the Malahat
to your mother's house—
the trees shuffling comfortably
through their silences,
the sun leaning like a confidant
over the highway—and it occurs to me I can tell you
anything. Is it the momentum of new love
or guilt or the autumn light softening the grasses?—
the wind's hushed remembrances and leaves
curling the diminutive arcs
of their spines, losing their summer poise.
I remember his eyes reaching mine and turning away,
the pressure of his thumb deepening on my skin:
you reinterpret the loss
not as an absence, but a presence,
and I fight with it—it's not the same
thing I'd have given you, given
the chance. And still brightness finds us
through the windows of your 1991
Plymouth Sundance, with its chipped white
paint and the red cushioned seats
warm with the separate small heats
of the bodies we belong to.

Strength in Two Parts

I.

One day it occurs to her that the words
don't have to be exact to be said
so when she wakes early in her childhood bed,
a sharp kind of courage is digging
in her body like a trowel
preparing for flowers or failure. June
in Northern BC. She goes downstairs
to wake her boyfriend,
groggy on the fold-out couch
he's agreed to sleep on
so her parents can pretend
that when the house is empty
they don't sneak into the bathroom
and shower together. Visiting
the parents, going to a cousin's wedding —
he'd signed up for all of this. And this too:
slouching up the stairs at seven in the morning
to sit patiently awake at the kitchen table
within earshot of the living room
where she stares at the squashy green armchairs
and tells her parents what
she couldn't tell them
before she knew he was waiting for her
in the next room.

II.

My father seems off for the rest of the day,
distracted. Mom is quiet too.
Silence after silence for so long
is too much—I have to get out of
the house, so we go to the art gallery.
The artist's notes encourage participation,
and scraps of canvas curl their edges
in a room set off to the side like a chapel
within a church. You watch as I draw trees and trees
in pure greens and purples and with long orange-
brown trunks and blue-shadowed branches
until the pastel is dust on my hands.
I forget the exact words
but somehow or other I told them
what that first boyfriend had done,
not to worry, I was okay now.
You drive us home in time for dinner.
Mom is in the kitchen
violently mashing the potatoes:
That. Fucking. Bastard, she says,
her breath just above tears.
You look around the kitchen, at the food ready
to be set on the table, and ask her
if there is anything you can do to help.

Sorrow Halved

I.

At her cousin's wedding, watching her boyfriend
lanky amongst the other well-wishers, it occurs to her
that parts of her sadness aren't hers anymore.
It's been divided, and though she's never been
good at math she's learning about
plenty: on the way here, her long-legged boyfriend
and her mother switched seats at the rest stops,
sharing the passenger seat next to her father
who insisted on driving the ten hours it takes
to reach Cranbrook from Prince George
in good weather. Her boyfriend is an anachronism,
likes the same music as her father. They know
the choruses most confidently, sing them loudly
so the notes fill the family vehicle: the turquoise 2002
Pontiac Montana she earned her practice driving
hours in when she was sixteen and afraid of speeding
tickets. In the backseat she woke to the voices
of her father and boyfriend singing some love ballad
and her mother laughing and watching for signs:
the kilometres flashing by, white font on green.
The things she's said now shared, split, frayed
into their loose ends — her heart
unknotted, unbroken. She remembers the drive
here and the things they haven't brought
up again, the other things she might've said,
the singing that carried on instead:
the bride's bouquet arcs
into her hands, unapologetically open.

II.

The bride and groom leave
for the Egyptian Suite and the hotel's
ballroom has wilted, white
tablecloths leaning lopsided
towards the floor. I hold calla lilies
in one hand, your hand
in the other. We walk my parents
to their hotel room—they're driving home
in the morning without us—to say goodnight
and the kind of temporary goodbye
that feels more poignant after
ceremony and change. Maybe that's why
the real conversation happens now,
their requests for details tentative
flourishes at the end of the day's
happiness. You squeeze my hand,
let go as I lift the flowers. Calla lilies
have a very, very faint smell—I press
my face to their centres. You explain
what I am too exhausted, just now,
to censor. And you know which details
will be most reassuring for them
to know: that you prevent me from having to
walk alone after dark, make sure you are
not working on the days I talk
to the counsellor who gives me labels
for things I don't like: *rape,*
abuse, anxiety. My parents look from me
to you to the bride's bouquet, searching
for a happy ending, for joy
doubled in the dim light of the hotel
hallway stretching out like a
long summer.

Love and Nintendo

Home for Christmas, I tell my brother
as little as I can: *He raped me.*
I just wanted you to know now.
A video game on pause on the basement TV,
colours muted. It won't occur to me
until later that it was several Christmases ago
that it happened: my first homecoming
from university, what might have been
the first of many long-distance relationship
reunions and what was, instead — well,
what it was. I don't know
the exact date — don't want that
kind of anniversary in my head.
It'd be worse than remembering
that first boyfriend's birthday each year.
I don't want, also, my brother to think
differently about me now, though
I know he will. He hides his face
with a pillow. *Do you have any questions?*
He doesn't. He sets the pillow back
down on the couch. We un-pause
the game. The TV's colours brighten.
We take turns being Mario. It'll be ages
before we run out of lives.

A Retinue for Mme d'Aulnoy

"One refrain continues throughout her tales: 'never has anyone seen anything so magnificent as this.' This 'never' that becomes 'forever' in her tales revealed her longing for a world different from the one to which she had been exposed."

—Jack Zipes in the introduction to Marie-Catherine d'Aulnoy's stories in *Beauties, Beasts, and Enchantments: Classic French Fairy Tales*

In the Tuileries Garden stands a statue of Charles Perrault.
Around him dance three children with clasped hands
and Puss in Boots with his large plumed hat. But I'm more moved
by Mme D'Aulnoy's White Cat, who mourned her enchantment
in a miniature black veil in a castle attended by bodiless hands,
a queen who out of necessity had grown comfortable with the macabre.
A statue of Mme D'Aulnoy should be set with her own cast
of characters: the White Cat, the serpent, the blue bird, the ram
with gilded horns. It should be lined with sugar almonds
and orange trees, and she should lie on a mattress
stuffed with phoenix feathers atop an intricate swell of river.
I sometimes tried to imagine what it would be like to hurt
the man who hurt me, but I have no heart for it. Mme d'Aulnoy,
though, she had a powerful imagination, a command
of folk tale motifs. More than Charles Perrault, she built
fairy tales up like turrets, turned the Parisian literary salons
into gatehouses. Through the reign of Louis XIV, she plotted
against the men who hurt her, abetted their murders:
schemed against her husband in the hopes an accusation
of high treason would kill him, helped assassinate
her friend Mme Tiquet's husband because he had abused her.
For a very long time, we have needed allies. Never has anyone
heard anything so true as this. She must have been so frustrated
by the paltry saviours available in her world when she wanted
a chariot drawn by winged frogs or unicorns dressed in gold
and driven, inexplicably and perfectly, by rose-coloured rats.
Never has anyone seen anything so magnificent.

Poem Featuring a 1994 Toyota Tacoma

For years I couldn't hear a Beach Boys song without
remembering the day in June that first boyfriend
drove us all the way from town to Bear Lake
with their *Greatest Hits* on repeat.
Too late heading out, the afternoon
already had a hint of orange about it
like the light of a camera
just before it flashes. The trees, rusted
with the lust of pine beetles, shivered
in the hot sky. The truck's shadow
flickered over the highway, dipped
into the ditches, darkened the dandelions.
Fireweed, purple and indignant, mimicked flame,
insisted it was a flower, not a weed,
insisted it was supposed to be there.
I stared out the window and concentrated
on not breathing, nausea rising
in my stomach as the truck's speed
pushed smoke into my face and hair.
He talked too little. I waited for him
to clue in, stamp the cigarette out, flick
the spark onto the highway. He didn't.
I'm angry, now, that I was silent:
we sped into sunset colours.
His hands were impatient
on the steering wheel,
and, later, I remember,
impatient with me.

Another Poem Featuring a 1994 Toyota Tacoma

He stole his father's truck again
to take me to see the fireworks: Canada Day,
red and white everywhere, maple leaves
painted across the round noses
of children, paper flags
sticking out of ball caps. And snaplight
glow bracelets, neon as angels.
I've begun to think divinity is
in ordinary things: gold-papered caramels,
paperclips, cold rain, the kitchen cabinet's fourth
drawer from the top, bright orange
underwear, blossoms… and, sweetheart, the way you
hold my body in the dark, your hand
on my belly. Looking back to that summer
I try not to blame myself, I try not to feel
stupid, but it seems so obvious, ominous,
now. I remember the traffic
around Fort George Park that night, smoke
left from the fireworks hanging like snakes
in the sky. And his father's truck sick
with the smell of cigarettes. And him
too quick with the gear shift, too heavy
on the gas. And the Beach Boys
still on repeat, chanting the joy of summer,
insisting we were gonna have so much
fun fun fun.

Love and Laundry

I could talk to you about how to get ink out of a shirt
and what temperature water I should use to wash my jeans.
I couldn't talk to you about what happened with that first boyfriend
because you just don't talk to your *mom* about *sex*
and I was embarrassed. I was more than embarrassed.
I was guilty. I suspected I was somehow a bad person.
I had tried to tell a couple of girlfriends over pizza
at a restaurant and they were mad at me
for letting him have sex with me. I know I didn't
explain it accurately. *Rape* isn't a word
that would have occurred to any of us.
They meant to be on my side
but being on my side wasn't much fun. I was sad.
They wanted to be excited about their own boyfriends
and trade gossip. I couldn't tell them
I missed him. I couldn't tell them I worried
I'd made a mistake. I couldn't tell them I wanted him back.
I wanted the idea of him but it was dirtied
beyond recovering. I didn't know if you would understand.
I skipped meals. I felt guilty about that, too:
you wouldn't have liked to know I wasn't eating properly,
taking care of myself. I felt very alone
and this, too, I suspected was my fault.
University was difficult. Being away from home
was difficult. Even doing my own laundry
was difficult but I was determined to handle it.
In fairy tales the princesses who don't have mothers
still need them and so their mothers manifest as doves
or hazel trees or rose bushes or gold-scaled fish;
the princesses are helped by these spirits because
they are inherently deserving. I was so unsure
of my own goodness I didn't think to ask
for more help. I understand now
you would have comforted me, of course,
you would have helped me
sort my lights from my darks, as always.

Minor Hockey

I was bored those weekends at the Kin Centre,
suspicious how our parents divvied up
their love for us. I didn't see why
I should sit in the stands cheering you on
when no one called out my name each time I lifted
my body off a bench and into my own endeavours—
I carried a righteous plastic blue suitcase
of wax crayons. I soon stopped watching your games.
I waited upstairs with the very hot hot chocolate
from the snack counter and sat at the fold-out tables
with my crayons and papers and explored
the places in the arena I thought only I knew how
to find: the edges behind the backboards, smooth
cement frosted over. I'd glide across in sneakers,
the crystals of ice shavings the Zamboni left
behind, rippled and refroze—treasures I didn't think
I could share with you as game after game
the tally on the refrigerator counted your *goals*
and *assists*. A measurable success that extended
into *penalties* that were supposed to make me feel proud
but I was the one who cheered and clapped
as the referees came onto the ice, circled
their elegant way into a respect for the rules. I don't get
hockey. I want everything to be fair: but it isn't,
that truth that slams against you like the away team
pushing you into the boards. I won't ask you
if the seizures felt like that, flattened out against glass
or ice, those hard visions you rarely mention
anymore. If the epilepsy hadn't
come, you really *could* have made it pro: I know
that now. You're not a sore loser but the old dream
must ache sometimes, the scent of skates
metallic over the imaginary ice, the trophies
silver neurons in your imperfect, gleaming brain.

Loyalty and Violence

When I finally told you that my first boyfriend
raped me, I was worried you would be mad
I hadn't told you sooner. You and Dad believed so innocently
that you could keep me safe that it was difficult
to tell you that you had failed. I wanted to protect
you from the truth that protecting someone is impossible;
I was half sick with the paradox of loving
men. When you nodded and said you were glad
I had waited to tell you I was relieved, and grateful.
You explained, *I think I am only just now mature enough*
not to hop in my car and track that bastard down
and hit him in the face. I know it is wrong too but
a part of me flushes with pleasure — not because
I wish pain on that first boyfriend but because
I enjoy the thought that I am worth fighting for.
It is an enjoyment, it occurs to me, suitably allotted
for a woman and is a kind of violence all its own.

Main Characters

I remember one evening in your car, that silver Malibu
with the 7-Eleven cups rolling in the back. You drove us
up Foothills, rounding our way back up to the Hart,
the radio crooning a cover of "Time of Our Lives"
and you told me you didn't know if you'd ever have what I have.
You were talking about love. I didn't understand.
The sun was setting in the same colours the pine beetles
had turned the valley, and that were curving in the glint
of the car's hood: a dry red that fell, too, through the windshield,
across your forehead. I sat silent in your passenger seat, guilty
for daydreaming about my boyfriend, the one
I knew then, already, I would marry. In the fairy tales,
there are never any weddings for two princes. I get it now.
Those silent years must have felt to you like those
the miller's daughter suffered when she could not speak
without dooming her brothers to be birds, or like
the pained quiet of the Little Mermaid whose tongue was cut out
because she loved the wrong kind of person, or of the eldest princess
who couldn't explain how she wore out her dancing shoes
or like something else I just can't understand.

Love and *Paradise Lost*

> Whatever pure thou in the body enjoy'st
> (And pure thou wert created) we enjoy
> In eminence, and obstacle find none
> Of membrane, joint, or limb, exclusive bars:
> Easier than air with air, if spirits embrace,
> Total they mix, union of pure with pure
> Desiring; nor restrained conveyance need,
> As flesh to mix with flesh, or soul with soul. (6229)
> —Raphael to Adam, Book 8 of *Paradise Lost* by John Milton

Raphael might be onto something—
spirits embracing, atoms lacing together.
What comes to mind are those photographs
from *National Geographic*, or
my old high school science textbook, the glossy pages
of galaxies being born—or no, dying—isn't it
that they are more beautiful when they are dying?
More colourful? Stars dying into each other,
angels trembling as they come. Just these
huge gaseous clouds red and pink and purple
rolling as if all of space
is a king-sized bed. Still,
it doesn't sound like as much fun
as what we do, does it? *La petite mort,*
the individual risks of desire—
I've never found
having limbs to be an obstacle,
and beneath or above or within our skin
I can still feel that other movement,
soul with soul, memorizing the paths
they'll take one day
when the rest of us is gone.

Everyday Aubade

for James, on the occasion of our engagement

> "If one has found true adult love, the fairy tale also tells, one
> doesn't need to wish for eternal life."
> — *The Uses of Enchantment* by Bruno Bettelheim

But this love makes me want forever
even more. More Monday night TV,
sour candy, summer and your hands
cool on my back, rain, mist,
more *buy milk on the way home*
and chocolate in gold paper.
And more nights like these:
your feet at the end of the bed,
pushing the sheets out of their folded
corners… Sleepless, tipsy
from the champagne—no, drunk
with decision—you tell me
how you knew you wanted this,
how extraordinary my specific death
will be for you. But you could die
first. It's the only way we imagine
leaving—last breath and the light
that separates us. It's 4 a.m.:
the new ring shines or doesn't shine
in its velvet box, the sheets
twist and warble on the bed,
you rub my naked hands
and we make promises in the dark.

IV
Blue Moon

Poem for the Father of the Bride

August 25, 2012

So certain of everything he had,
and then his life glittered in front of him:
hot salt flashing as it fell over him,
heavy in the hollow chemical drum
he'd been trying to clean
from the inside. The heat
almost lost him, the weight
of it collapsing on his skin—
burns on his body and how many,
exactly, broken bones?
What was left visible: just his one arm
raised above the metal drum, white
as the salt, white as a flag
of surrender.

He learned to walk again. His burns,
shiny patches of skin on his shins
and shoulders—which never quite
straightened. He nurtured a love
of box-mix brownies he learned
to assemble during that year of mending
that changed his marriage,
opened into the possibilities
that led to me—this dress white as salt,
surrender, and his arm reaching out
for more.

Poem for the Mother of the Bride

As soon as you zipped me into the off-white gown
with the tiny Swarovski crystals, a dress so like
and unlike all the dresses I ever imagined
as a child — English lace netted over creamy taffeta
down into the scalloped edge, the long train,
the fabric's flounces — I became aware
of my overactive bladder. And so
I crowded into the tiny bathroom with you
and you held my gown up for me while I peed.
I'm not embarrassed by my body and you aren't
either. My body is just a place I live in, as you live in
yours. Although of course I lived in yours too. Mom,
on my wedding day I felt as I was supposed to feel,
more beautiful than ever before, and more loved,
but it was not the narrow, focused love of a fairy-tale
union. When I think about the story of Thumbelina's
coronation, how she meets the king of the flowers
and is presented with a pair of gently curved wings
from a white fly, I wonder how the story could be
so wrong. It opens with a childless woman
who so longs for a child that she pays a witch
for a grain of barley that grows into a tight tulip bulb.
With the sentimental intricacies of magic, the woman
kisses the petals and the flower gives a bang and opens:
and there, on the tiny green stool in the centre of the tulip,
is her new daughter. There is a certain romance
to the way you tell the story of my own birth
and it makes me feel protective, too, of Thumbelina's mother
and her long-awaited joy. What she must have gone through
when Thumbelina went missing. Oh, I know Thumbelina
went through a lot — so many undesired suitors and near-escapes —
but why did she never send word? How could she have been so
thoughtless, so ungrateful? The day she married the king
she couldn't have felt with her new wings the way I felt
standing in the bridal room with you smoothing the folds of my skirts.

Poem for My Brother

Though it was Gretel who wept and whined
for home and Hansel who bit his lips and held
her hand, who hummed and hugged her,
though it was Gretel who wept and whined
for home and Hansel who went hungry,
his pockets slowly emptying of bread
the birds stole in the dark, their wings
directing them home, and though it was Hansel
who bit his lips and held his sister's hand,
hummed, and hugged her, though Hansel
was the big strong boy who wanted to —
bless him — protect his frightened sister,
it was Hansel locked in the birdcage
who stopping humming, and little Gretel who swept
the small cottage, who stoked the fire,
who pushed the enchantress into the oven,
who lived the rest of her life with the fragrance
of burning flesh and gingerbread in her nostrils.

Love and Long Drives

She learned from her parents to stay awake
in the passenger seat on long drives, on late-night drives —
to keep her eyes on the road, a courtesy
to the driver who might get lonely,
wide-eyed in the extending glitter
of the road lines in partial moon,
weak headlights. Or who might get lulled
by the silence a long afternoon that seems to pull itself
from the dawn. Stay awake. The girl remembers
her manners into her new love: the young man
behind the wheel. And then years go by
and she forgets. Hours from their last rest stop,
she wakes: *I'm sorry,* she says with the guilt
of the well-slept passenger. *Meant to keep you
company.* The vehicle hums. *Don't be sorry,*
he says. *I like it when you fall asleep
when I'm driving. Makes me feel like you feel safe.*

Blue Moon (Honeymoon)

I spent too much money on an ivory lace
dressing gown that you appreciate very much,
untying the sash round my waist
slowly. You kiss my bare stomach
and leave the bed, carefully fold
the fragile garment over
the back of the hotel room's plush red chair
before returning your attention
to my skin, and mine to yours
and both of us trying to believe
in the magic of ceremony
and detail, feel out a difference, a change
in us, our bodies, newly married love—

It's a blue moon tonight. Remembering
the lunar eclipse years ago, the red moon
you held me under, you expect indigo,
royal, peacock, sapphire. I explain, no,
the moon is just the full moon,
second full moon in a month, pearl
as always, white... Disappointed,
you dress anyway, join my hand
with yours in the sleepy elevator,
step past the plastic tropical ferns in the lobby,
through the sliding glass door
and into the midnight air beside the lake
to stare up at the familiar moon,
perfectly ordinary and rare.

Love and IKEA II

Those days you left work early
and newness clothed us like light — as though the candles
from the wedding dinner were un-extinguished, still gold
above our plain cotton sheets. But ordinariness comes
so quickly: some usual illness saps me,
the long hours at the office pull the light
even out of your short blond hair, the eyebrows
I always tell you made me love you.
Deadlines push against the windows
of the apartment. I ask you what we should name
the spider who lives in the bathroom — Lady Leroy,
Rosalie, Leanne? Her small body has a sheen
mine doesn't anymore. We thought we knew
enough about the improbabilities of happy endings
to make our own. We were not naïve, we were
prepared and hopeful, and then last night
someone mentioned someone else's extra
ten pounds, someone else mentioned the dust
at the corners of the warped laminate flooring,
the dishes, the ants marching in from the un-gardened
garden, the chair that needs mending, the unfolded
clothes. Everything seemed so terrible I couldn't stop crying
and then you punched the coffee table,
the stupid birch-effect veneer thing
that matches the bookshelves. It's solid, this knowledge
that we won't ever be a match for the world's
petty colds, long winters, unsolvable loneliness,
but IKEA furniture is barely real. I stood stunned
at the fist-shaped dent in the tabletop, flecks of burgundy
in the pressboard's jagged cracks. You hadn't really
hurt yourself, I knew, and when I arrive home tonight
the argument is gone: a new coffee table,
identical to the old one. It only cost $40
to replace it, you explain: *I'm sorry.*
I didn't want to live with it.

You just want me to stop crying.
You want newness to glint in us
like old light. I want these things too.

Intersection

At 8th and Alder, a gentleman in rumpled denim
beautifies the corner store's lawn with a raucous
weed whacker. The smell of grass and dandelion leaves
is shredded into the soft wind and blown across the street,
past a brick apartment building where paramedics
lift a stretcher into a van the same shiny red
as the wet poppies in a neighbouring garden. The body
is covered in a white sheet that I know — without
touching it — is pilled, much-washed and thin.
The aggressive regular song of the weed whacker
is incongruous with the paramedic's work, almost
blasphemous, but only because I forget that death, too,
is ordinary. Here: the slant of the road,
the stop signs, the clipped roses, the poppies
gently nodding with old rain, the obscure light
of hydrangeas and mild traffic. A small monkey figurine
pokes its wire-and-bead head out of a planter pot.
Three women in pale, crisp pantsuits
meet on the sidewalk to introduce each other
to their dogs: a golden retriever, a toy poodle
and a young beagle who investigates the strangers'
pockets for pleasures. The grey sky
is warm with indistinct clouds.
Last night we made love for the first time in too long;
I had expected I would be happy all day today.

I'm suffering from depression and you

want to install a night light in our bedroom
to help chase the shadows away. But
darkness stands in for a fear that is irreparably rational:
everything ends. I cannot stop thinking
how much I have to lose and so certainly. My friends,
my parents, children we haven't yet conceived
but who come to me, flickering like green leaves
beaten off a tree by hard early autumn rain.
I want to pull faith around me like a feather-
filled duvet but worst-case scenarios untuck the sheets
from the corners of the bed. My feet are cold
and the room is moonless. Of course you want me
to stop crying beside you. Of course enlightenment
can happen in the dark. In bed
we close our eyes and let gravity
pull us, individually, towards sleep, towards
the centre of the earth. If we move
towards the centre of each other,
it is another force, less scientific. I can hear the rain
pulling summer down from the trees outside;
here, your hands rustling to reach the extra blanket.

On Learning a Girlfriend Started Cutting Again

The news comes gently into my week
with a tidy, *thought you should know* email,
full of *I'm okay* and *the doctors are recommending
medication this time*. I read her words, and the words
are just regular words. *It's not anywhere near
as bad as the last time, but enough I have a few stitches,
appointment with a psychiatrist, new prescriptions.*
The words behave as words do
on a computer screen: they wobble, ever so slightly,
because it is the end of the day and I am already tired.
I imagine her boyfriend coming home from work that night
to find her as she was: to find that love, even good love,
is not enough against winter, the world, its sadness
shapeshifting into spring rains.

                                  Days later she arrives
at our party with a bag of potato chips and a generous smile
and a wide silver bracelet on one wrist, conspicuous,
cool, tender, and I watch the way her boyfriend
watches her — delicately, not possessively — and the room
is filled with what I can only describe, honestly,
as goodness or as love and it is a soft thing, goodness,
and I suppose it must go hand in hand — forgive me —
with hardness. That old metaphor of only seeing light
against the dark. I do not know if we can understand
what softness is without the contrast of what hurts us.
Goodness could be mistaken as a quality of light.
The kitchen's fluorescence is buzzing
like our recollection of bees, and, sweetheart, it falls
into your shoulders like honey: I wish
we knew this sweetness couldn't spoil.
The old building has shifted into the slope
of the city, the patio door is ajar and the night sky
leaks its aching in. It makes me remember
poetry from second year university, a line
about heartbreak I wanted desperately to understand:

It is like the keening sound the moon makes sometimes,
rising. The professor told the class, then, to think
about what the poem meant, *because of course*
the moon doesn't actually make any sound, and I thought—
I was eighteen—what does *she* know, the moon
might very well make sympathetic noises and isn't the universe better
for thinking that it does? I wanted to know other people
who were like poets and could hear the keening sound
of the moon, hurting with the effort to rise.
It was the music of the spheres I wanted,
not blood, not anyone's wounds.

*

Among the other guests I watch her boyfriend
touch her elbow, bring her another drink, glance
at the corner of her mouth. I glance there, too,
as if my looking might have some effect on the gravity
of her lips, floating upwards on her face.
But I could never be an astronaut.
I can't handle being a day's drive from those I love—
I could never learn to live so far away from their planet,
even if the distance made its fond songs, its blues,
suddenly more audible. Standing on the earth I don't know,
I hear the humming of these fluorescent kitchen lights,
the ceiling lamp in the living room
with one of three bulbs burnt out. Charms tinkling from
the wine glasses relatives chose from our wedding registry—
how long have we loved each other?—
the crunching of potato chips, the crinkling of plastic bags
emptying into tin bowls.

I know the boyfriend is the first who's ever been gentle
to her: I won't think about the other men. I didn't know them.
But I know her love, now, is good. I recognize their hands
like ours were in our new-love years, touching
each other's shoulders and arms as if touching
the horizon, smoothing a sunset lake into its separate colours.

Months ago they arrived late for dinner
because they'd come to the restaurant via the park
and they couldn't help themselves, needed time
to pluck grass out of her long blond hair, smooth down
the wrinkles in his shirt — kisses had pulled them into the trees,
onto the ground, and they glowed from beneath their skin
so that looking at them, across the table, we could intuit
their bones as phosphorescence upturned
in the water of their bodies. I remember noticing, then,
the specific quality of light in the Japanese restaurant,
and your hand on my knee, wondering if happiness
could ever be described as *complete*, if our own bones were burning.

*

At this small party of potato chips and old friends,
I want to imagine that her having good love,
having a boyfriend who touches her because
he knows she would like to be touched
rather than only because he wants to touch her,
is enough to fill the gap inside her:
but her bones can be glowing
and still she can fill with rain, rivers
that wash her skeleton clean, drain
its heat. I have also felt evaporated,
even hovering above the love of my life. Slowly,
you filled a dotted-line silhouette like a prince
from one of those sticker albums
with collectible cards I kept as a child.
Tonight, our first-floor apartment flickers
with light. I want to peel this moment
off the back of this night
and press it onto a page. Keep it.
Keep it even though
I didn't want to know, didn't want
to be reminded: into my life again,
ungently, comes the knowledge that love,
even good love, is not enough to soothe

the kind of brokenness that can hear
into the keening sound the moon makes
sometimes, how it echoes beautifully
in circles in the silver bracelet around Naomi's wrist.

On Fairy Godmothers

Sometimes, when my mother returned to the kitchen
in the evening to rediscover the dirty dishes
hadn't been cleaned yet, she would sigh and say,
I guess my fairy godmother is being lazy tonight,
and then she would snap on her yellow rubber gloves
and scrub the cast iron frying pan
and the pot that wouldn't fit in the dishwasher.
It didn't occur to me she could have bigger wishes
than clean dishes and it was comforting to know
that she could make them come true herself
with a little lemon-scented dish soap
and some extra time.

January Is Terrible So Far

She accepted a ride back home from a family friend
she met at a Christmas party. He seemed nice.
Invited himself up. Helped carry her bags.
Then stayed for hours with her, stayed
in ways that mean she'll have to relearn that touch
can be good. I receive this news over the phone.
My friend is crying because this happened
to her girlfriend and she doesn't know how
to help and she's sorry to call me so upset so stop her
if she's talking too much and I can't handle it
but she didn't know who else to call
or anyone else who'd know best what her girlfriend
needs right now. I recite the standard things against
infection and pregnancy, trauma and self-blame.
Insist how possible the healing journey is,
but the length of it unfolds in me
like an impossibly long, rumpled area rug,
a tripping hazard, and I'm angry she has to make it
at all. How many years before I could
make love in the dark without being afraid
you would magically transform into someone
I didn't want to know and couldn't see.
How many years before my friend's
girlfriend can hear someone say *slut*
and not feel it echo in that family friend's voice
above the bed she felt she'd die in. I don't want
to be melodramatic, but when you arrive home
from work tonight with a bouquet of yellow lilies
and daisies dyed purple — their centres
stained an odd turquoise — it seems like a miracle
that anything helps.

Two Poems for Dortchen Wild

Dortchen Wild, who lived next door to the Grimm family in
Cassel, contributed thirty-six tales to *Children's and Household
Tales* before she was twenty, including "All-Kinds-of-Fur" about
a princess who flees from the father who wants to marry her and
finds safety disguised in another kingdom. She and Wilhelm
Grimm were eventually wed in May 1825 when she was thir-
ty-one and he was thirty-nine.

I.

In the same letter she admits she has a crush
on her best friend's older brother, Wilhelm,
a thirteen-year-old Dortchen Wild writes
about attending a large baptismal party.
It is the autumn of 1808. She cheerfully explains to Lotte Grimm
how she forgot to bring her sewing bag to the table
and was forced to sit politely with her knitting needles
and one completed sock. I am delighted to read
that she successfully stole an extra piece of cake
by hiding it inside the knitted sock.
I, too, always want more sweets than I'm given.

II.

I will restrain myself from any proclamations
about the nature of truth. History leaves out
so many details. Fairy tales do too, but
I prefer them. In the 1819 edition of the tales
Dortchen is a "Wild deer," a veiled reference
from her lover who, scholars suggest, wished
to offer her a gift: she told Wilhelm Grimm
the story of "All-Kinds-of-Fur" and it was rushed
to the printers in October 1812. The 1819 edition
with her hidden name, the insinuation of her body
graceful as an animal leaping on light hooves,

adjusts the story so it is clear that the princess
marries her beloved and not her father the king
who wanted her. The father-king
and the bridegroom-king were different men.
In the fairy tale, true love diverts disaster.
In the history, the details are not known
but it is easy to believe that something happened
to her between 1812 and 1819 that made it impossible
for her to be sweet and merry for many years.
I do not understand the world I live in.
It is easy to believe that bad things happen to women.
It is why I want also to believe that Wilhelm
took her secret and his instinct was to magic it away
into a book and then wait patiently — as you must do
for a terrified deer — until she could trust again.

Love and Impatience

You'd like me to be more spontaneous.
You'd like to make love while the syrup
for my handmade caramels bubbles unattended
on the stove and the smell of dark butter
sweetens in the air. You'd like to make love
in the morning, and in the afternoon.
You'd like to make love in the evening
until the sound of the falling rain seems
to come from a world we won't really
have to return to or learn to understand.
I get impatient with myself, too. It has been,
as you say, years—I should be over it. When my body
panics in response to your wonderful hands
I get sad for both of us. You get frustrated.
Oh, you hold me until I stop crying but also
you explain that you don't think we should have to
worry about this anymore. You think it's unfair
that something that had nothing to do with you
and so long ago now should punish you, but this
is how it is: I will never completely get over it.
Sometimes your touches will make me flinch.
But sometimes—and you must remember this—
we can kiss forever and nothing bad happens. Not even
burning; we saved that batch of caramels
before they blackened. Spent the rest of the afternoon
wrapping them in tiny squares of waxed paper,
our fingers nimble and light and sweet.
I will never get over that, either. I promise.

Fitcher's Bird

There is a German version of "Bluebeard"
in which the bride discovers the room
of disembodied limbs and white faces,
and she recognizes them as her lost sisters.

Unlike Perrault's heroine—who opened
the door to her forbidden room and dropped
the little key in blood and whose curiosity
is betrayed by its stain and who is only saved

by the timely arrival of her brothers
to rescue her from her husband's scythe—
the bride in the German tale conceals
her knowledge of her husband's evil

and tricks him into believing her compliant
while she secretly sews her sisters
back to life; at the end of the story the bride
not only lives but she rescues the women

who usually stay in that terrible locked room.
I would like to have that power.
To walk away from harm but also
to help mend those whose stories are so much

more grim than my own. I loved a girl from high school
who went missing for two years
while I was off at university falling in love
with feminism and an intelligent man

with beautiful eyebrows. She had gone away
with a man much older than her who
promised her a house and a marriage
and babies—the happily ever after

she and I had dreamed up during our sleepovers
of curling irons and nail polish
and the feeling that there was something faintly
dangerous about wanting sex. This man

did not deliver. Nothing was as it appeared —
not the houses or the cars with lapsed payments
and fraudulent leases or his declared intention
to love her gently and with grand gestures.

In the fairy tale, the evil man is a sorcerer
who only has to touch a beautiful girl
to compel her to jump into his basket
so he can carry her to his house glistening

with gold and silver and a basin of blood.
At first, amongst such riches, each woman
must believe she has everything she could want.
At first she must be happy.

I do not know for how long my friend
believed in the life that older man gave her,
each new city, new start, new debt,
new ways of being touched and being hungry.

The bride in the fairy tale smuggles her sisters
out of the terrible shimmering house
and instead of preparing her husband's supper
she dips herself into a barrel of honey,

cuts open a bed and rolls in the feathers
until she looks like a magnificent bird.
It is impossible to recognize her.
She does not need wings to walk out

of that house and come back home.
I do not know how she knows this
or why it is true for her
and not for so many others.

When I Dreamed I Did Not Dream Of You

A lot has been made of true love's first kiss,
but most of that is Walt Disney's doing.
He framed the princess's story with the expectation
of a rescuer: he gave Snow White a prince to dream about
from the beginning. Down by the wishing well she dreams,
and sings, and dreams, and sings, and her dreams
are dreams of hoping to be found by a man. How
technically advanced Disney's animation, how natural
Snow White's body's movements, how ingenious,
the woodland animals, the previously anonymous
chorus of dwarves individualized into Grumpy, Happy, Sleepy,
Bashful, Sneezy, Dopey, Doc. It must have seemed romantic
to imbue the prince with the power of true love's first kiss.
But in the Grimms' story it's not a kiss that awakens Snow White.
Only a chance misstep, a stumble, brings her back to life:
one of the prince's servants trips over a shrub
while carrying her coffin away from the dwarves' mountaintop
and the jolt frees the piece of poisonous apple from her throat.

This is at once less and more disturbing to me:
the prince in the original story is less important,
perhaps he has less power,
but also he has never before seen Snow White.
He begs the dwarves to let him take her
body away to his kingdom so he can cherish
the sight of her in her glass coffin.
We're never told what Snow White thinks of all this:
she's wed to a stranger who would have been content
to worship her perfect beauty had she never opened her eyes,
or her mouth, if her chest had never risen again with breath.
Our first kiss was sweet and nervous. You kissed me—
a peck on the lips, really—because I wanted you to. I suppose
you noticed I was beautiful. You knew I would never be silent.

Poem for My Body

No one else rescued me. Not my father
or my brother or, years later, the gentle man
who became my husband. Not my mother
or my best friend or any of the women
who listened to me tell my story
and told me their own stories as we drank
cups of hot chocolate in cafés in Vancouver
while outside the rain poured and fallen leaves
gathered like audiences in the streets. No.
None of them were there that night
when that first boyfriend leaned over me,
against me, into me. I remember how I froze,
how I could not move and I thought I hated myself,
hated my body — because it paralyzed me that moment,
because it was not beautiful enough or it was too
beautiful. But I do not hate my body. No.
I will love it. Let me praise my eyes for crying,
my throat for crying out. My hand, its impulse,
the red slap it left across his face.
Let me praise my arms for gathering my clothes,
my legs for taking me out of that house,
my feet for remembering left for brake, right for gas.

On Learning My Dearest Cousin Is Engaged to Be Married

I remember how we pretended to be twins, though you had freckles
and I had none and your hair had an auburn tinge
while mine was simply dark; we begged for matching outfits
and posed for photographs with our faces hiding behind books:
We're the same! We're the same! we chanted,
though you had more courage and I was less raucous. We lived
in a fairyland crafted out of the wild blueberry
bushes those summers at our grandparents' cabin
and held hands as we watched for evidence of bears;
Grandma told us to sing if we wandered off
so the animals would hear us coming and leave us alone.
In the fairy tale, though, the bear comes to the cottage
and asks if he can warm himself by the fire, his shaggy black head
trembling like the soft cloth of a magician's hood:
*Children, would you mind beating my fur a little
to get the snow off it?* And the girls fetch a broom
and sweep the snow off the bear's wet fur and giggle.
The bear puts up with all kinds of mischief from the girls—
they tug his fur and walk on his back.
Nudged by her sister's boldness, the more timid Snow White
kneads the bear's fur, thinks she sees gold shimmering
through the bear's dark coat. She isn't completely sure,
but she moves towards love, reassured by the sideways glances
from Rose Red's laughing eyes. Those ungraceful years
of high school, I was buoyed by the anonymous
Valentine I received in eighth grade, proof that
someone out there thought I was beautiful.
The night before my wedding you confessed
you were the one who sent that Valentine
because you knew I had been feeling sad.
I don't know why I was surprised. Snow White
married the black bear with her sister's blessing
and a fairy tale rewards goodness, so there is, of course,
another bear, and Rose Red, too, falls in love,

unafraid of his growl. She's full of song,
summer staining her fingertips with blueberries
and darkening the freckles across her cheeks.

Victoria Day

Almost musical pauses in the rain,
the droplets on the still surface of the ocean,
silver sounds turning into rings. The afternoon
smooth, not seamless — tiny stitches
in the wobbly harbour horizon,
a tear, a trill, a call. I want to hold

your hand and trust tranquility, the sky's
second world shaken by gentle
weather. Another comfort —
a pair of ducks unconcerned
by our presence. I imagine our affinity
to anything coupled... What's here is
a kind of grace, God in the green smell
of spring, the opaque scent of wet rock,
warped wood. I crouch down on the dock
for a closer look: the two ducks,
male and female, noiseless
in companionable circling,
two privacies nudged
together in soft grey rain and uncertain
reflections: and I am just thinking how much
I love you when the sudden curve
of the otter's body appears,
a shining length of fur
that rises with a violent splash, snaps
the drake's neck and drags him
under.
        White feathers
on the water busying itself
with smoothing things over.
The female startled away, solitary
somewhere else.

Schloss Steinau, Hesse, Germany

The Grimm Brothers grew up across the street
in a half-timbered magistrate's house:
studying Greek and Latin, collecting eggs
and not thinking of magic. By all accounts
it was the best time of their lives. It is quiet here, calm,
unburdened by tourists and noise except
the gentle twittering of small, silver-winged birds.
Watching you squint in this particular light,
it occurs to me that most magic
in fairy tales is the kind that hurts, that traps
and twists and isolates — the happily ever after
is the return to the disenchanted life,
the confidence that love is enough. This must be
the solace those brothers sought to return to:
the nostalgia of afternoon sunlight on the castle
that stood in the neighbourhood of their childhood.
Strawberries from the market stain our hands.
I can feel this picnic turn into memory
even as I busy myself with worry about my white sundress.
The light is carefree, like a prince
just transformed from his animal skin or
a princess newly awakened — giddy
with the reward of ordinariness.
Through no fairy intercession that I know of,
you are young and beautiful, and I am too,
and strawberry juice runs in rivulets down our wrists.

Pigeons

In London pigeons bluster around
the underground's faregates, flutter ankle-deep.
They adorn the heads of statues,
the stairs of St. Paul's, scatter
into the air around the dome, patterning
the day with their scuffles. The stairs
of the cathedral soften in the centre
of each stone step, a history of feet
in semi-dark. We climb the stairs
and I wonder if all vacations, no matter
their confessed purposes, are about looking
for God, finding a better view
on this world. From the dome's balcony
the pigeons' high-sky scattering seems
less destined, somehow, than
it appeared when they lifted off
the ground—it's hard
to follow anything, even you,
with my eyes.

Ravens

> "If the ravens leave the Tower, the kingdom will fall... "
> — Common English superstition

I sometimes wish you were as tame
as the ravens who have not abandoned
the Tower of London — have not, will not,
cannot survive outside captivity now but may
successfully breed. Their wings clipped
so they will stay within the walls of the castle,
the fairy tale. Their large satin bodies, feathers
black as the centres of your eyes, which open on me
in those moments in bed when we most need
to know each other. How does any known thing
— sound, sight, love — travel from one person
to another except through the air between us.
Let's call all air, all the space between us, *sky*
so we can let it settle over us in the bedroom,
breathe it out now across the Tower Green,
its evenly cut grass glossy with light.
I stand and look and wait for a revelation
of love and death and history to reward me
for being here, in a place so old. Nothing.
Calm. The sun warms the back of my neck.
You kiss me gently below one ear.
Your bare arms circle my waist
like a low wall, a safety. I am happy
watching the ravens prospering quietly
with human attention, the hidden sheen
of my wishes ruffling like feathers.

Swans

> "For many years scholars debated the issue of whether the slipper was made of *vair* (an obsolete word for 'fur') or *verre* ('glass'). Folklorists have now discredited the view that the slipper was made of fur and endorse the notion that the slipper has a magical quality to it and is made of glass."
> — Maria Tatar, *The Annotated Classic Fairy Tales*

I want to endorse magic, too. Beyond the murmur
of the crowds, the glint of security staff badges,
the grand apartments at Versailles hum elegantly,
as if someone is pressing wet fingers on the rims
of crystal glasses. Just a little pressure
can make very fine things sing:
Charles Perrault invented Cinderella's glass slippers.
He also said that Versailles *is rather a world*
where we see assembled varied miracles
drawn from the great universe. Our universe
is bigger than it was in the reign of Louis XIV,
its miracles brighter and more brittle, pigments aged
against oxygen and our expelled breaths:
so many of these miracles can be damaged by a camera's flash,
the accumulated weight of every perceptible sigh —
portraits, polished silver. Even stone. Magic
is fragile. You lead us through. Self-guided,
we hold each other's hands until they get too sweaty,
then break apart. It's August. An August that presses against
the arcaded windows overlooking the gardens,
the marble pilasters — multicoloured marble —
crowned monograms, chandeliers like stars gone sentient
with glamour. The Hall of Mirrors is,
momentarily, for us: it divides our images
into benevolent rectangles, cuts across my bare shoulders,
your almost-shy smile. Time collapses, all gold
is gestural, and a secret hallway connects
the king's apartment to the queen's bedroom: her bed
is draped in burgundy, pink, plush floral. Each gilded capital,

each letter deliberately gold-dusted as if by an approving
godmother. Sculptural figures lift candlesticks into
the air cleft by shadow and the flourish
of reflected light and fleur-de-lys —

These are fairy-tale rooms.
These are the kinds of rooms in which Cinderella's shoes
echoed. But we're wearing Birkenstocks.
We're tourists. We love each other sincerely, painfully,
self-consciously, obviously. And here,
between the shining floors and domed ceilings, velvet ropes
make almost everything inaccessible to us — the embroidered beds,
the gold and glass and marble. Everything is marked off,
history delineated, artefacts explained on plaques.
My hair won't stay out of my eyes
but I see you, the smudge of sunscreen on the back of your neck:
uncomfortable amongst the regal stones, painted analogies,
the heroes and their tranquil angels, you roll your shoulders back,
adjust your backpack, shift your weight from one foot
to another, one foot to the other.

Outside, the mateless swan at Marie Antoinette's Temple of Love
begs for the tourists' attention. The reality of it,
the imperfect white of its feathers, the solitary s of its neck,
ornate as any gilded character, seems to announce
that the world is less an assembly of miracles
than a place where we see assembled varied instances of loneliness.
Pastry crumbs litter the grass, tufts of lost feathers,
ticket stubs, crumbled tissue. I grab your hand and squeeze.
You squeeze back. Later, we'll get locked in
the park, stay too long at the edge of the Grand Canal.
The sky will double in the water and trail after us.
We'll catch a train back to our tiny Paris apartment where the sky
will take up so much space it will feel there is
not enough room to make any more love. Now,
we watch the swan lift its wings, shuffle,
dismiss the sky, then settle on the ground,
as if hoping it will become something else by midnight.

Blue

We were fighting. Raised voices. It was bad enough
that I decided to leave the apartment,
so we stood in the doorway, dramatically not saying

how crazy we are for each other, me on one side,
you the other, me staring at the warped laminate flooring
of our apartment, you at the faded, dust-saturated carpet

of the hallway that leads out into the street. I remember this
imperfectly — the variegated browns of our surroundings,
dull as the plumage of a female mallard. But

from my vantage point I must have been able to see past you,
to the fireplace and the wall you once painted for me —
bright blue, a surprise I came home to one day,

the living room the same fragrant hue that Chagall's bride
floats into, that strange, luminous midnight sky
of a new marriage. I didn't look past you, though —

listened to you say something scary,
or something that seemed scary, a generalization
about our love or how it worked or didn't,

something unsympathetic to our walks by the water,
the way we watch the ducks circling each other
like brushstrokes blending into the light. I remember

wringing my hands, pulling one hand back and forth
over my arm, looking at the divide between us,
the flooring, the carpeting, the slender silver runner

of the doorway. Suddenly realizing
I was holding my house keys, I'd raked their teeth
across my skin, made it bleed. And so

I had to cross back over and you led me
to the medicine cabinet, dug out the Polysporin,
and the healing started again.

Creatures

Into her marriage she brings a large unicorn blanket
she could not part with, though it embarrasses her
that she still frets over judgement
from a beast she knows is imagined.
Her husband loves her and cannot bring himself to hate it.
The pragmatic part of him notes that the blanket
is at least warm and lies smoothly over the goose-feather duvet.
The woman lies beneath the blanket beside her husband and is comforted.
Long before she learned to be angry,
a part of her had mourned the unicorn,
convinced it would know just from looking at her
that she was no longer worthy.
Though her family and friends couldn't fathom her secret
if she didn't speak of it, a unicorn would see her body,
an un-jewelled thing amongst the birch and pine,
and it would be ashamed.

She had found it easy to believe that she was mundane
and could no longer be a friend to magic. Now, the wind sings
into the un-blossomed tulips of their garden
as the couple edges toward the dark forest of sleep.
The woman has learned to stop blaming herself
for a violence she once thought had ruined her heart.
At night the unicorn leaps out of the threads of the blanket
and lands gently outside the bedroom window
to lower its horn in the slant of the moon.
It might approach to nudge against their skins.
It knows instinctively how the man and the woman
hold their pleasures, like sugar cubes, inside their hands,
and it has always approved of such tenderness between creatures.

April 17:

Rain drops crowned the white tulips
and they glittered so impossibly bright
in the grey downpour I almost felt
that any one of them would stretch
its graceful leaves in my peripheral vision
and reveal herself to be a fairy, shake the water
out of her hair and tiptoe animated dust
across the sidewalk. It was childish, of course.
I know that the universe is expanding,
that everything alive is mortal. I know, too,
that if I hadn't said *white*, if I had just said *tulips*,
you would have imagined the wrong thing,
wouldn't you? When I think of tulips
I think yellow, red, pink. You probably think
these things too. It's okay. Language is so often
imprecise, so much like love — I just want you
to know the tulips this morning were white,
with the improbable postures of ballet dancers,
flickering under the hard rain, and
for one moment their colourlessness was magnified
like shadow in cut glass and I believed in magic again,
for one second, before I turned away
back into a world where buses were tunelessly
rolling through the blackening puddles
and songbirds were seeking shelter somewhere else.

On Reading the Fairy Tales Recently Recovered from the Municipal Archive of Regensburg, Bavaria

I.

It occurs to me that each story began with someone,
though it's easy to think they have always existed
in our collective consciousness to pass from one hand
to another, like warm clay fingerprinted by time
and the private dust of bodies elongated
by desire, the future. These new stories remind me
of the first need — for invention and metaphor, to see
the world as it isn't. I need to see windows instead
of puddles when this city we love in just rains and
rains and rains. I need the same comfort as those who first
spoke fairy tales aloud as if they were spells.
Franz Xaver von Schönwerth recorded these stories
as faithfully as he could, no poetic flourishes or polish,
and they seem even closer to the original storytellers
than do the romantic revisions of the Grimm Brothers
I have loved since childhood. These stories are full
of surreal plot twists, seven-league boots and leaps
of logic, gratuitous vengeance and marriages
consummated early with unapologetic flair. Perhaps
we have more in common with magic than we think,
sweetheart. Perhaps it's worth looking more closely
at the puddles on these streets, the world reflected
backwards beside our forwards-going feet.
So many stories are strange.
So many surfaces are capable of reflecting light.

II.

The weasel with fur as white as snow might turn into a prince
if she offers him an egg to eat; its shell
might harden into pure silver and make her rich.
A king might be obliged to hide his golden hair
in a dirty kerchief and find work as a gardener,
but she might recognize his goodness
because of the bouquets of roses he hand-ties
with strands of his hair. The mermaids keening
with desire, languid in the transparent dresses
of their midnight bodies, will float through
the window to lie on the curtained beds,
but might be consoled if she throws ripe plums
into their cool hands. The hazelnut branch
her father brought for her might turn into gold.
She might be transformed into a white calf
but her mother will find and restore her.
Her brother might have the strength to kill a nine-headed giant.
Her mother-in-law might be a witch but
will eat suckling pig instead of her heart.
If she writes down her wishes with a quill
made from the feather the crow offers her
she might never be hungry, and if she pulls
the rusty nail out of the wall and places it under
a turnip she might know true love. If she sprains her ankle
and lets a dung beetle fly her to the doctor
her life will turn around. If she finds a red silk ribbon
she should take it, if she keeps her hair tied out of her eyes,
if she really looks at things, if it occurs to her
that which is ugly may be beautiful, the world
might puddle with magic — she might feel it reverberating
with the wide steps she takes, her huge leaps of logic.

Book of Alternative Services

The priest asked us to kneel,
draped his stole over our clasped hands.
I trembled so much it shook off our fingers
before all the blessings were spoken.
The photographs don't show that,
just the long veil falling over my gown
and the solemn nape of your neck.

Three weeks ago I spent a dollar at a florist's
on an unlabelled bulb I expected to be a paperwhite.
I've grown them before, the first a gift
from your mother years ago in a shallow glass vase.
Easy to care for, even early, even in winter.
This one's been growing by my windowsill,
keeping me company like the cat I can't convince
you we should adopt. (*Can't fool me*, you say,
what you want is a baby and we've got these student loans…)
Its green shoot stretched like a curious neck —
last night I brought a fingertip to its head
and could almost feel it purr, feel the pulse
of it making up its mind: this thing that doesn't
wait for anything, that I wait for.
This morning I see it's not what I expected.
Pink. It's supposed to take weeks and weeks
to chill a tulip bulb, to force it to bloom indoors,
there are rules, a process I didn't follow,
but here it is: what it was, it was all along.

When I tell your mother, she suggests I've got
the magic touch: it's February and I'm willing
to believe almost anything — and I do,
I do, though those aren't the words we promised
each other. *The Book of Alternative Services*
uses *I will* in its wedding ceremony. *Will you
take this woman to be your wife? I will.*

Your answer so emphatic the congregation
laughed. Fond groom. O, that future tense,
I do, I will, every day
I will. Weeks before, when we talked
with the priest, he asked if we wanted to omit
the old-fashioned blessings for the fruits
of the marriage and we declined. Yes
to fruit and flowers, yes to magic,
yes to touch, yes to paperwhites
and yes to white and gold and green
and pink, to this tulip that's taking its time
and yes to the cat from the avenue over
who sometimes scratches at our patio door
to be let in.

Author's Notes

Fairy Tales

"On the Bicentennial of the Grimm Brothers' *Kinder-und Hausmärchen*": Jacob and Wilhelm Grimm published the first volume of their *Kinder-und Hausmärchen (Children's and Household Tales)* in December of 1812 and the second volume in 1815. The collected stories have been widely influential and bicentennial celebrations took place worldwide between 2012 and 2015. The city I reference has undergone a change in spelling: although the city I visited while writing these poems is now spelled Kassel, during the Grimms' lives (and until 1928) it was known as Cassel.

"Love and IKEA": The song quoted is "I Want to Know What Love Is," a 1984 song by Foreigner.

"Little Brother": This poem borrows heavily from "Little Brother and Little Sister," a story included in the fairy-tale collections by Jacob and Wilhelm Grimm.

"Waiting for Spring, or Something": In most Christian liturgical calendars, Epiphany is the celebration of the Magi visiting baby Jesus and the revelation of God the Son as a human being. It takes place on January 6.

"Folk Tale Type 425C": The statue referred to in the poem is housed at the Louvre in Paris, France: *Psyche Revived by Cupid's Kiss* by Antonio Canova. Tale type 425C: "Search for a lost husband" is one of many tale types listed in the Aarne–Thompson tale type index, a multivolume listing used by folklorists to identify recurring plot patterns in the narrative structures of traditional folk tales.

The Princess Who Felt the Pea

"Briar Rose": "On the very day that the princess turned fifteen, the king and the queen happened to be away from home, and the girl was left all alone. She wandered around the castle, poking her head into one room after another ... She put her hand on the spindle."

— "Briar Rose" by the Grimm Brothers, translated by Maria Tatar

"Lavinia": In William Shakespeare's *Titus Andronicus*, Titus's daughter, Lavinia, becomes the object of an argument of possession. Although Lavinia is in love with and betrothed to Bassianus, Saturninus (Bassianus' older brother) tries to make a claim for her. Eventually, Lavinia is married to her true lover, Bassianus, but on her wedding day he is killed and she is gang-raped; her tongue and both hands are cut off. She spends the rest of the play as a pitiful background character until her father "mercy" kills her. She bears resemblance to "The Maiden Without Hands," a figure found in many stories but perhaps most notably in the Grimm Brothers' fairy tale of the same name.

"The Swans' Sister":

"Their sister wept and asked, 'Can't you be set free?'

'We don't think so,' they said. 'The conditions are too hard. You'd have to go six years without speaking to anyone or laughing, and during this time you'd have to sew six little shirts for us made of asters. If just one single word were to fall from your lips, then all your work would be for naught.'"

— "The Six Swans" by the Grimm Brothers, translated by Jack Zipes

"The Third Eldest Sea Princess":

"The next year the third sister went up above. She was the most daring of them all, and that's why she swam along a wide river that flowed into the sea… "

— "The Little Mermaid" by Hans Christian Andersen, translated by Tiina Nunnally

"The White Bear's Bride":

"After she went to bed and put out the light, a man came and lay down beside her. It was the white bear, who cast off his pelt during the night. She was never able to set eyes on him, because he never came in until after she had put out the light, and he was up and about before the sun rose."

— "East of the Sun and West of the Moon" by Peter Christen Asbjørnsen and Jørgen Moe, translated by Maria Tatar

"Donkeyskin":

"In her dying hour the queen said to her husband the king: 'Before I die I want to make one last request of you. If you decide to remarry when I am no longer… '

'Oh,' said the king, 'don't worry about that. Rest assured that I would never in my life consider remarrying.'

'I believe you,' the queen replied, 'Your love and devotion prove that to me. But just to be absolutely certain, I want you to swear that you will pledge your love and remarry only if you find a woman more beautiful... than I am.'"

—"Donkeyskin" by Charles Perrault, translated by Maria Tatar

"The Frog Princess": Although in popular culture it's believed that the princess kissed the frog to transform into a prince, in the original story it's an act of violence that frees him.

"The princess became really annoyed, picked up the frog, and threw him with all her might against the wall ... When the frog fell to the ground, he was no longer a frog but a prince with beautiful, bright eyes."

—"The Frog King, or Iron Heinrich" by the Grimm Brothers, translated by Maria Tatar

"The Giantess": In "Jack and the Beanstalk," most widely circulated by Joseph Jacobs, the giant's wife hides Jack from her husband.

"The Princess Who Felt the Pea": In Hans Christian Andersen's story "The Princess and the Pea," the princess proves her true nobility when her sensitivity is revealed; she notices the lump of a single pea beneath twenty mattresses and twenty featherbeds. At the end of the story, "the pea was sent to a museum, where it is still on display, unless someone has stolen it" ("The Princess and the Pea," by Hans Christian Andersen, translated by Maria Tatar).

"Beauty": Although beast-bride stories exist (and I recommend seeking them out), the beast-bridegroom story is more commonly known. In North America the most famous animal-husband story is the French variant, "Beauty and the Beast," popularized by Jeanne-Marie Leprince de Beaumont. The heroine must see past the ugliness of her suitor, the Beast, in order to earn her happily ever after.

"Rapunzel":
"Rapunzel had long hair, as fine and as beautiful as spun gold. Whenever she heard the voice of the enchantress, she would undo her braids, fasten them to a window latch, and let them fall twenty ells down, right to the ground. The enchantress would then climb up on them to get inside."
— "Rapunzel" by the Grimm Brothers, translated by Maria Tatar

I would also like to acknowledge Donna Jo Napoli's novelization of Rapunzel's story, *Zel* (1996), which in part inspired this sonnet crown.

Learning to Be Two

"Hans Christian Andersen's Self-Portraits": In addition to his writing, one of Hans Christian Andersen's many talents was the creation of intricate cutouts. Using only a pair of scissors, he cut figures out of paper that resembled the kinds of fairy-tale characters with which he populated his stories.

"A Retinue for Mme d'Aulnoy": Marie-Catherine d'Aulnoy was married off to a baron thirty years older than her when she was only fifteen. After bouts of intrigue and exile, she settled in Paris and helped to popularize literary fairy tales — she used them as a commentary for her dissatisfaction with the oppressive, aristocratic lifestyle of the time.

Blue Moon

"On Learning a Girlfriend Started Cutting Again": The poem quoted is "Privilege of Being" by Robert Hass, from his collection *Human Wishes*.

"Two Poems for Dortchen Wild": The story "All-Kinds-of-Fur" is about a king who lusts incestuously after his daughter following the death of his queen. The princess flees from her father in a disguise to another kingdom; in some versions she hides her beauty with a cloak of many furs and in others it's an animal skin. I allude to the French variant earlier in the poem "Donkeyskin." For more about Dortchen Wild and the other women behind the Grimm Brothers' fairy tales, I recommend the wonderful little book *Clever Maids: The Secret History of the Grimm Fairy Tales* by Valerie Paradiž.

"Fitcher's Bird": "Fitcher's Bird" is a variant on the murderer-husband story that most people know through "Bluebeard," the French version that Charles Perrault included in his fairy-tale collection. "Fitcher's Bird," like many other stories, was originally told to the Grimm Brothers by their neighbour and family friend Dortchen Wild, who later became Wilhelm's wife.

"When I Dreamed I Did Not Dream Of You": *Snow White and the Seven Dwarves* was released in 1937 by Walt Disney Productions, the first full-length cel animated feature film and the first Disney animated feature-length film. Disney's adaptation of the fairy tale for film led to many changes of the genre, the influence of which is still very much felt today; many of these changes (as noted by Jack Zipes in his essay "Breaking the Disney Spell") seem to emphasize the role of the saviour/prince and on opportunities to experiment with new visual techniques rather than expanding a community of storytelling.

"On Learning My Dearest Cousin Is Engaged to Be Married": This poem borrows heavily from the fairy tale "Snow White and Rose Red" by the Grimm Brothers.

"Schloss Steinau, Hesse, Germany": Steinau was the childhood village of the Grimm Brothers. The village boasts a Renaissance-era castle only a short walk from the house where the brothers grew up, which is now home to a museum that commemorates the brothers' lives.

"On Reading the Fairy Tales Recently Recovered from the Municipal Archive of Regensburg, Bavaria": This poem refers to Maria Tatar's English translations of Franz Xaver von Schönwerth's stories, recently published through Penguin Classics as *The Turnip Princess and Other Newly Discovered Fairy Tales*. Von Schönwerth did not embellish his stories or try to smooth out their narratives in the same way that his contemporaries the Grimm Brothers did, so they retain a closer approximation of their oral tradition flavour.

"Book of Alternative Services": *The Book of Alternative Services* is the contemporary liturgical book used alongside *The Book of Common Prayer* in most parishes of the Anglican Church of Canada.

Credits

Most of the poems in this book first appeared in journals, magazines and anthologies, sometimes in slightly different form. My thanks to the editors.

The sonnet crown "Rapunzel" received an honourable mention in the 2013 Young Buck Poetry Prize Contest with *Contemporary Verse 2*. "Fire and Safety (or, If my little brother is jumping out of helicopters into raging flames I don't want to know about it)" won the 2014 Young Buck Poetry Prize with *Contemporary Verse 2*.

"The Third Eldest Sea Princess" was longlisted for the 2012 CBC Poetry Prize. It was later published in *Grain* magazine. "Folk Tale Type 425C" and "On Learning a Girlfriend Started Cutting Again" also first appeared in an issue of *Grain*.

"Waiting for Spring, or Something" was longlisted for the 2013 CBC Poetry Prize. It later appeared in *Event* magazine, along with "Love and *Paradise Lost*."

"Lavinia" was shortlisted for *Arc Poetry Magazine*'s Poem of the Year in 2015. "Sorrow Halved" was also published in *Arc Poetry Magazine*.

"I've never read a love poem" was first published in *Echolocation*.

"Book of Alternative Services" and "I'm suffering from depression and you" first appeared in *Dappled Things*.

"Poem Featuring a 1994 Toyota Tacoma" and "Another Poem Featuring a 1994 Toyota Tacoma" first appeared in *Dreamland*.

"Beauty" was first published in *Rose Red Review*.

"Love and IKEA II" and "January Is Terrible So Far" appeared in *The Maynard*.

"You're Living in a Big City Now" and "April 17:" were first published in *The City Series: Number One – Vancouver*, Frog Hollow Press (2015), ed. Michael Prior.

"Briar Rose" and "Donkeyskin" were first published in *Blue Unicorn*.

"Blue Moon (Honeymoon)", "Swans" and "Blue" appeared in *Qwerty*.

"The Giantess" was published in *The Antigonish Review*.

"Love and Impatience" was published in *Synaesthesia Magazine* in their excellent BODY&SEX issue.

"Poem for My Brother" was first published in *Gingerbread House Literary Magazine* under a slightly different title, "Poem for a Protective Brother."

"Fairy Tales," "Dust," "Love and Nintendo," "Creatures," "Everyday Aubade," "On Reading the Fairy Tales Recently Recovered from the Municipal Archive of Regensburg, Bavaria" and "Schloss Steinau, Hesse, Germany" were all originally published in issues of *Room* magazine. "Loyalty and Violence" was also published with *Room* as part of their *No Comment* project. "Love and Nintendo" is also part of *Resistance*, ed. Sue Goyette, forthcoming with Coteau Books.

Acknowledgements

Thank you to Rhea Tregebov, Natalie Morrill, Laura Ritland and Sue Sinclair, whose editorial insights enormously strengthened this book. Thank you to Keith Maillard and Joelle Barron, who also read poems at key stages of the writing process.

Thank you also to the many mentors and peers who encouraged my writing and directly or indirectly helped this book into being: Lorna Crozier, Tim Lilburn, Carla Funk, Steve Price and George Sipos. Thank you to Sierra Skye Gemma, Jeffrey Ricker and Elise Marcella Godfrey for comradery, shared meals and encouragement. Thank you to Alison Bougie, Matthew Pixton and Naomi Gehrels, true friends and believers in magic.

Thank you to my colleagues and my former students in Vancouver at the Bolton Academy of Spoken Arts, who indulged me in discussions about fairy tales and reaffirmed their importance to me over and over again. Thank you to every writer and friend who came to my reading series, Swoon, and fostered a dialogue about love and literature. Thank you to new friends who welcomed me into the Okanagan literary community.

Thank you to Vici Johnstone and everyone at Caitlin Press for their support of the project. I'd also like to mention that this work would not have been possible if not for the great wealth of scholarship about fairy tales currently available. Among many others, all of whom I can't possibly name here, I owe a lot to the writings of Maria Tatar, Jack Zipes, Marina Warner, Valerie Paradiž, Robin McKlinley, Kate Forsyth, and Donna Jo Napoli.

Most of all, thank you to my family, who makes my "happily ever after" so complex, rich, messy and magical. Dad, I love that twinkle in your eyes. Mom, thanks for the love of books and the copy of *The Annotated Classic Fairy Tales* that started my critical investigation into these stories. Darrell, I don't know where I'd be without you along for the adventures. James, this book was always for you. Now it's also for our sweet Rose, and for the little one we haven't met yet. I love you. I'm so lucky I get to share fairy tales with all of you.

Author Bio

Ruth Daniell is an award-winning writer whose poems have appeared in *Arc Poetry Magazine, Grain, Room* magazine, *Qwerty, The Antigonish Review* and *Event*. The recipient of the 2013 Young Buck Poetry Prize with *CV2* and the winner of the 2016 Nick Blatchford Occasional Verse Contest with *The New Quarterly*, Daniell is also the editor of *Boobs: Women Explore What It Means to Have Breasts* (Caitlin Press, 2016). She holds a bachelor of arts degree (honours) in English literature and writing from the University of Victoria and a master of fine arts in creative writing from the University of British Columbia. She lives with her family in Kelowna, BC.